MW00979231

FLOWERCHILDREN

Text and Illustrations by BRIGITTE BROCATO

Enjoy reading —

Brigitte

ISBN: 978-0-692-48999-4

Copyright © Brigitte Brocato 2010

Copyrights Library of Congress Washington D.C. TXu 1 - 724 – 279

October 19. 2010

KINDNESS IS A SPECIAL ART

THAT EVERYONE SHOULD KNOW BY HEART

This book is dedicated to my beautiful granddaughter

LEAH ELIZABETH BROCATO

Thank you Leah for inspiring me to write this book.

Once upon a time, far away from the noise of the big city, there was a lovely magical garden. 🍂

In this magical garden was a big apple tree. Butterflies fluttered, ladybugs climbed on flowers, and snails slowly made their way across the meadow.

Here lived the most beautiful flower girls in all the land; their names were:

They were inseparable and played all day in the magical garden. Every afternoon the flower children had a tea party and gossiped, giggled and had a lovely time. 🍃

One day while they were having fun at their tea party, Leah noticed a small figure hiding behind the apple tree. "Look girls," whispered Leah, "I think there is another flower girl in our garden."

Pia and Mia looked curiously at the small, fragile flower girl. She looked so sad and pale. "What is your name, and why do you look so sad?" asked Pia. 🍂

"My name is Gia and I am very sad because my dress and my petal flower hat have no colors. All you girls have such beautiful green dresses and petal hats, but look at mine, just ordinary and plain, no colors."

Leah replied, "Don't be sad Gia, I know how we can make your dress and hat just as beautiful as ours. We simply paint them." Gia smiled and said, "You are the most wonderful friends, thank you!"

Leah explained, "We only need three colors, they are called basic colors. These colors are red, blue and yellow. We will mix them and create new and different colors, they are called secondary colors."

The flower girls got busy collecting flowers, roses for the red color, bell flowers for a blue color and buttercups for the yellow color.

They put all the baskets with the flowers in the grass, picked some leaves for mixing the colors, and then they looked for feathers to use as brushes for painting Gia's dress, hat and shoes. 🍂

Leah explained, "When we mix blue and yellow, we will create a new color, a secondary color."

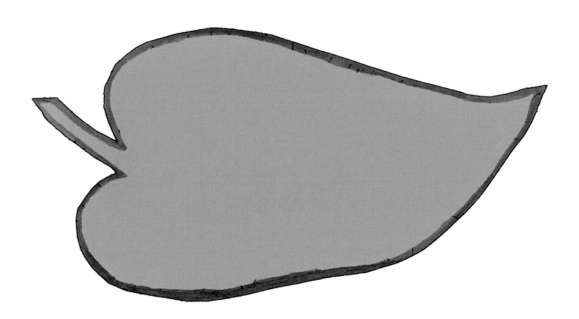

"This color will be green."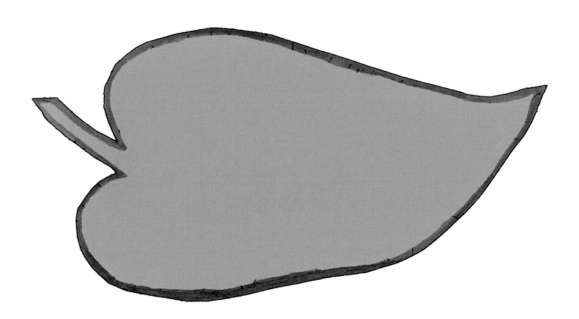

"Then we will mix the red color with yellow and what will we get?"

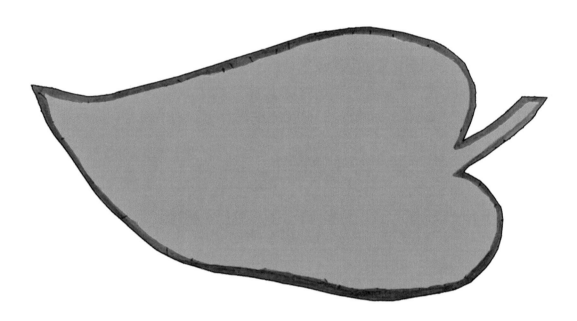

"We will have an orange color. Secondary colors are so beautiful." said Pia.

Mia added, "Now we will mix the color red with blue…" 🦋

"to make a purple color," and so they did.

They used the feather brushes to paint Gia's petal hat with a dazzling orange. They created a beautiful green color for Gia's dress and a bright orange color for her hat.

Her plain dress became a vivid green, and her slippers a lovely purple. Gia simply looked beautiful. She looked as lovely as all the other flower girls. 🍂

She spent all of her days playing with her new friends in the magical garden, where butterflies were fluttering, birds singing along and all the little magical creatures in the garden gathered to listen. They played music...

...went horseback riding,

...played croquet,

...and they danced.

They lived happily ever after in this wonderfully enchanting magical place.

Other books by Brigitte Brocato

ABC -- Available in English and German

Waldy -- Available in English, French and German

From most major online book retailers

Contact the author at brigitte.w.brocato@cox.net

CPSIA information can be obtained
at www.ICGtesting.com
Printed in the USA
BVXC01n1351290317
479327BV00002B/4